HORSEPOWER

CHOPPERS

BY MANDY R. MARX

CAPSTONE PRESS
a capstone imprint

Blazers Books are published by Capstone Press,
1710 Roe Crest Drive, North Mankato, Minnesota 56003
www.mycapstone.com

Library of Congress Cataloging-in-Publication Data
Library of Congress Cataloging-in-Publication Data is available on the Library of
Congress website.
ISBN: 978-1-5435-2462-8 (library binding)
ISBN: 978-1-5435-2470-3 (paperback)
ISBN: 978-1-5435-2478-9 (eBook PDF)

Summary: This text discusses choppers and their unique features.

Editorial Credits
Hank Musolf and Jessica Server, editors; Kyle Grenz, designer; Jo Miller,
media researcher; Kris Wilfahrt, production specialist

Photo Credits
Alamy: Agencja Fotograficzna Caro, 17, Ian Shipley BKS, 27, K.L. Howard, cover,
picturesbyrob, 11; Capstone Studio: Karon Dubke, 9, 13; Dreamstime: Afroto,
20-21; Fotolia: lefty, 14-15; Getty Images: Alexey Bubryak, 28-29; Newscom:
akg-images, 19, Ingram Publishing, 5, ZUMA Press/Matthlas Oesterle, 24;
Shutterstock: Ljupco Smokovski, 23, Pressmaster, 6

Design Elements
Shutterstock: hugolacasse, khun nay zaw, Shacil

Printed and bound in the United States.
PA017

TABLE OF CONTENTS

ONE OF A KIND RIDE

A chopper is a motorcycle built to personal taste. Just like people, no two choppers are the same.

Choppers are usually built from scratch. Some people build their own choppers. Others hire **experts** to build bikes for them.

expert—someone who is very skilled at something or knows a lot about a certain subject

A **custom** paint job adds the finishing touch. Many chopper owners want a flashy paint job that attracts attention.

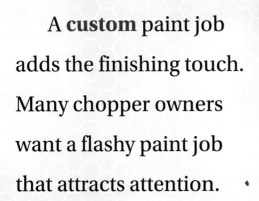

custom—specially done or made

CHAPTER 2

CHOPPER DESIGN

Choppers are built to go faster than most motorcycles. They are also meant to look like no other bike on the road.

Many choppers have **lightweight frames**. A lighter frame makes the bike quicker and easier to handle. Some chopper frames look like thick skeletons.

lightweight—not heavy

frame—a basic structure over which something is built

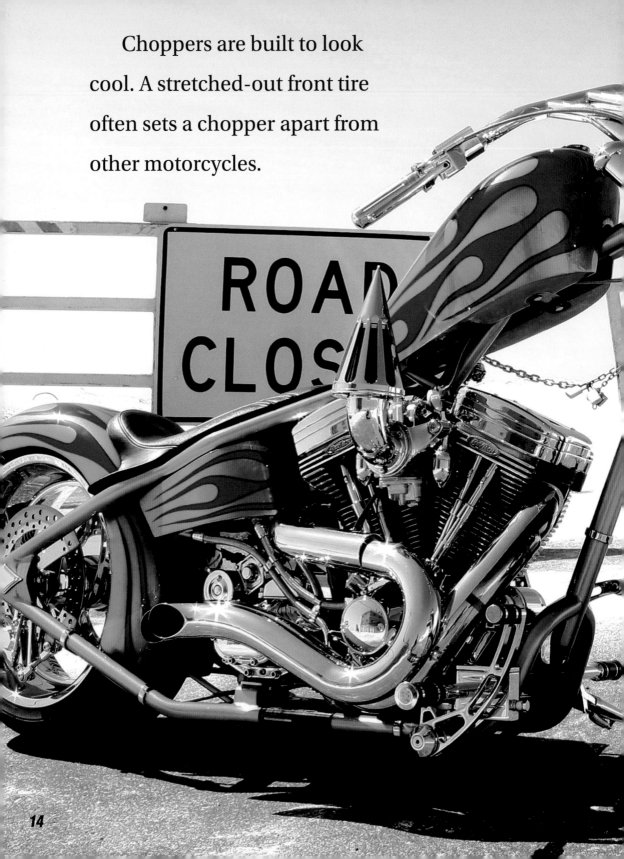

Choppers are built to look cool. A stretched-out front tire often sets a chopper apart from other motorcycles.

If the front tire of a chopper is stretched out too far, the bike will tip.

CHAPTER 3

PERSONAL TOUCHES

Custom bikes reflect the style of the owner. Many people like choppers better than regular motorcycles.

A paint job gives each chopper its own look. Some people paint their choppers to show their interests or beliefs.

Choppers gained popularity in 1969, when the movie *Easy Rider* came out. The bike in that movie had an American flag theme.

CHOPPER DIAGRAM

ENGINE

CUSTOM PAINT

EXTENDED FRONT TIRE

CHAPTER 4

CHOPPERS IN ACTION

Choppers seem to fly down the open road. Some choppers can reach 120 miles (193 kilometers) per hour.

Chopper owners share the thrill of riding. They join chopper clubs and hit the road together.

Chopper owners love to show off their bikes. They take them to motorcycle rallies around the world.

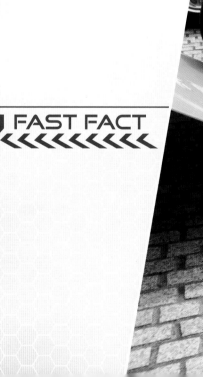

FAST FACT

J.C. "Pappy" Hoel held the first Sturgis Motorcycle Rally in South Dakota in 1938.

READY TO ROLL!

GLOSSARY

custom (KUHSS-tuhm)—specially done or made

expert (EK-spurt)—someone who is very skilled at something or knows a lot about a certain subject

frame (FRAYM)—a basic structure over which something is built

lightweight (LITE-wayt)—not heavy

READ MORE

Bodensteiner, Peter. *Choppers*. Gearhead Garage. Mankato, Minn.: Black Rabbit Books, 2017.

Lanier, Wendy Hinote. *Choppers*. Let's Roll. Mankato, Minn.: North Star Editions, 2017.

Monnig, Alex. *Behind the Wheel of a Chopper*. In the Driver's Seat. Troy, Mich.: Momentum Books, 2016

INTERNET SITES

Use FactHound to find Internet sites related to this book:

Visit www.facthound.com

Just type in 9781543524628 and go.

INDEX